Ethel's Girl

Ethel's Girl

Recollections of
A Cajun Childhood

Rosemary Bernard Groves

The Hummingbird Press
Winston-Salem, North Carolina

Copyright © 1992 by Rosemary Bernard Groves
Printed in the United States of America
All rights reserved
ISBN 0-9621194-4-x

Book design by Stratford Books

Second Printing, 1994

To my father, Roger Landry Bernard,
and to my sisters and brothers,
Jeannine, Phil, Irma, Donald,
James, Ruth, Gordon,
Michael, and Kevin.

Contents

Preface	ix
Into the Darkness	3
Hey, Red, Need a Ride?	6
No Gray Lines on My Soul	10
Stealing Dolls at the Church Fair	18
Ruby Falls	21
Chocolate Mush and Biscuits	31
A Dollar for Your Little Girl	37
Mrs. Dupuis	39
How the Day Goes	45
Don't You Know Birds Can't Talk?	48
Mama's Gift	51
God's Gracious Clover	61

Preface

My sisters—Jeannine, Pookie, and Ruthie—and I were in Houston for a once in a decade get-together, a time for making connections, sharing memories, and talking about Mama. I do not recall exactly what I said that touched off Jeannine's explosion, only that I had once again tried to defend Mama—who had died two years earlier—against criticism the likes of which had been aimed at her all her adult life.

"Rosie," Jeannine said in exasperation, "she was no good! Mama was no good. No one cried at her funeral."

I do not know if that was true. I cannot say that no one cried. I know I did not cry. All our lives Mama had been larger than life, the focal point of everything, the caller of all the shots, but when she died there was no void where she had been. She just was not there any more.

Why, then, have I, over the past two years, felt compelled to write about Mama? To be sure, she was extravagant, lustful, and eccentric. She was funny, though she did not know she was funny. She was a highly intelligent, aggressive businesswoman who ran her properties from her bed because, as she put it, it was easier to lie down than not to lie down. She was one of the most profoundly lonely people I have ever known. She could not believe in God—at least she said she could not—but she believed in the power of traiteurs, the folk healers of Cajun life. And she believed in St. Anthony, the Patron Saint of Lost Things. With a traiteur and St. Anthony, Mama felt that she was covered. This may be the stuff of which "The Most Interesting Person I Ever Met" articles are made, but it does not begin to explain my need to write about Mama. For in truth it is not about Mama that I need to write; it is about Mama and me.

Mama hurt me more times than I could possibly recall. She hurt me in places so deep that only in recent years have I begun to plumb their depths. Even now I live with the shame she brought on me and our family. Yet, thirty-five years after I ran away from home, sitting in a hotel room in Houston, Texas, I defended her. Why? What was there about her and my relationship with her that leaves me feeling alternately humiliated, ashamed, disgusted, proud, angry, grateful, and guilty? I do not know. This much I know: I was afraid of her (I never got over being afraid of her), yet I needed her love and approval the way any girl needs the love and approval of her mother. And this I know as well: writing these stories and essays has diminished her grip on my life.

I had been telling some of the stories for years. Throughout my adult life, I had recounted tales from my childhood and youth, especially the more bizarre ones about Mama, to friends and acquaintances. Invariably, people found the stories "interesting," "entertaining," even "amazing." But as time passed, I felt less and less inclined to tell my stories. They did not create empathy in the hearts of their hearers. To the contrary, they created a distance between me and the people to whom I told them. After hearing one of my stories, one person said, "You don't tell people that, do you?"

So, I stopped telling my stories.

Some stories I had kept to myself all along, so shameful were they. A few stories I kept even from myself.

Then in the winter of 1990, a deep clinical depression overcame me, and I no longer had the mental strength to keep the memories submerged beneath the level of consciousness. Old stories, new stories, forgotten stories, buried stories, unknown stories began bursting to the surface of my mind like beach balls which I could no longer hold under water.

When the memories began flooding my mind, I ran—

literally—to the word processor and began recording every recollection, every thought, every feeling. Sometimes tears flowed. Sometimes I wailed, the pain was so great. Sometimes I burst out laughing as I recalled childhood events which had been rendered irretrievable when I indiscriminately shut off myself from my past. Writing was therapy for me, prescribed by myself, an effort to exorcise demons, some of which had been trapped inside my head for forty years.

Only later, after reading some of this material to very close friends, did I realize its potential for bringing healing to others as well as to myself. Some of my friends—most of whom were women—wept, all of them were moved. The pieces reached deep inside and touched my shame to their shame, my pain to their pain. That is when I decided, with the assistance of my husband, to put the stories into publishable form.

A few words about these pieces. First, they are my stories; they are not the stories of my nine brothers and sisters. Each of us experienced growing up differently. My recollections of events surely differ from their recollections; my interpretations of the meaning of things differ as well. I do not say that my recollections are correct and theirs are not. I say only that my recollections are my recollections.

Second, the pieces are memories; they are not histories. They may or may not be descriptive of what really happened. I have no way of knowing. The capacity of children to understand the motives and complexities of adult life is limited. Nonetheless, it is important that we pay attention to our memories, because we are shaped by our recollections of the way things were.

Finally, the stories and essays are not intended to constitute an autobiography, even though they are arranged more or less chronologically. An autobiography suggests a life which can be discerned from beginning to end. The following series of pieces, uneven, leaving large gaps in the telling of my story, is a more accurate picture of where I am. I am in the process of remembering my past, gathering up the dismembered pieces, and putting them together as one puts together a puzzle with no picture to go by. A form, an outline is appearing. I like what I see. There is hope in that.

Rosemary Bernard Groves
Winston-Salem, N.C.
September, 1992

Acknowledgements

I wish to thank my husband Richard for editing and critiquing these pieces, but mostly for believing in me.

I also acknowledge the good work of Bynum Shaw who took the initiative in publishing this work. Without him, it would still be in the directory of the word processor.

Ethel's Girl

Into the Darkness

I had seen it before, though at first I could not remember when. Five years earlier, Charles Leblanc, husband to my oldest sister Jeannine, had rented an outboard motorboat and had taken my husband Richard, our boys, and me riding in the Atchafalaya Basin, that haunting watery forest of moss-cloaked cypress which drains hundreds of thousands of acres of swampland into the Gulf of Mexico. Now adult and an officer in a utility company, Charles proudly showed us places he fished when he was a boy growing up in French-speaking south Louisiana.

We had tired of winding down serpentine bayous and had turned on to a broad straight channel cut through the swamp by an oil company that came to drill in the Fifties, when we spotted it, over on our right, standing like a decrepit praying mantis, propped up shakily in death. An elevated walkway, tree-top high, wooden, two-boards wide, with a railing on each side. Its supporting pilings were sunk in the mud and marsh grass thirty feet below, and its nearer end concluded in a ladder which descended to a landing near the water's edge. Charles pulled the boat over and tied it off so we could take a closer look at this rickety curiosity whose very existence seemed to require some sort of explanation. Richard said that he would like to go up on top and take a look around, and since neither Charles nor either of our boys dared to accompany him, against my better judgment, I said I would go, too.

Our brief walk on the decaying walkway was unsettling in a strange and terrifying way. The boards creaked with our every step. The railings gave way at our touch and dared us to put our weight on them. The entire structure groaned and swayed as we walked gingerly along its spine. Below, the swamp waited in all its stagnant mystery. Ahead, a hundred yards or so, the footbridge disappeared in a shroud of Spanish moss and overhanging limbs and foreboding darkness. With every step I felt that I was being enveloped by something amorphous and evil, closed in, my way of escape cut off. Finally, I told my husband that I was afraid and that I was going back. I knew he would think I was silly, but I did not care. I ran back to the ladder, my jolting steps sending palpable vibrations down the spindly legs of the creature into the murky earth. When I reached the landing, I looked up and saw Richard climbing down the ladder above me.

The strange swamp walkway existed only in my memory and in a photograph Richard took while on top—until I saw it a second time.

It was late afternoon. Dark clouds swirled overhead and the wind cried through the cypress. I was alone on the landing. There was no boat behind me, no way of escape. I climbed the ladder because I had to. The horny backs of alligators broke the surface of the water below, and cottonmouth water moccasins slithered over knobby cypress knees. Once on top I saw only the darkness into which the walkway disappeared, and I walked toward it. I did not look back. It was not in my power to turn around and to run away. The creaking of the boards was muffled in my ears, and the wind which swayed the tops of the trees around me did not touch my skin. I was drawn inexorably to the darkness. Soon it enveloped me, drawing me into its silence. The light and the storm disappeared behind me, and I reached my hand into the void like a blind woman reaching awkwardly for a familiar wall. I felt a cold round knob which I knew I must grasp and turn. As the door opened, a slit of light rent my darkness from top to bottom.

I pushed the door open and looked into Aunt Lynn's kitchen, shining and white, clean, smelling of the morning's coffee, the leftovers of which I knew were in a jar in the refrigerator. Aunt Lynn, sweet, troubled Aunt Lynn. To her I had run when in the fourteenth year of my life I could no longer resist the ugly truth that Pookie and Jeannine and Phil forced on me, and I ran away looking for someone to be a mother to me. From her I had run four years later when the church closed its mind to my questions, and I found another home for my soul and my body.

I knew that neither Aunt Lynn nor my cousin Ray was home, but I felt as comfortable and as welcome as I had thirty years before when her kitchen was my kitchen and her home was my home. Everything was as familiar as when I left, when I had to leave—the cabinets which reached the nine-foot ceilings; the calendar with the picture of the Sacred Heart of Mary; the well you could see out the back door, in earlier years a working source of water, but in my teen years a home for Uncle Voorhies's gold fish. It was all just as I had left it.

Peanut butter and syrup. That is what I would have eaten if it had been a fall afternoon in 1959, and I had just come from Mt. Carmel High School, an energetic and bright sixteen-year-old at home at last. That is what I would eat now. The bread and the peanut butter and the Steen's Pure Cane Syrup would be in the pantry just as they were in that beatific sophomore year. The pantry, on the left of the counter, had two doors, hinged on the outside, and handles together in the middle. I took the handles, one in each hand, and pulled the doors open. There, so close I could feel her breath if she had any, was Mama, her casket upright in the pantry, her red hair flared out, her hands folded in death, her eyes, cold and glaring at me in life!

I woke up screaming.

I cried all day.

Hey, Red, Need a Ride?

At twenty-seven years of age Roger Philippe Antoine Bernard was still unmarried. It was unusual in the closed Cajun culture of the late 1930s for a man his age not to be married. In Roger's case there were reasons.

In 1913, when Roger was five years old, his father Leon shot himself in their home in the country south of Lafayette. Roger's mother, Irma Landry Bernard, stumbled over her husband's body in the living room. She held his head in her lap as he died. Irma never remarried. She continued to live on the family farm, caring for Roger, his older brother Jerome, and his sisters, Evelyn and Marie Louise. In 1928, fifteen years after his father's death, Jerome hanged himself from a tree in the front yard. Some time later, a fire destroyed the house, and Irma moved with her three beleaguered children to a house in town.

Roger never recovered from the tragedies of his childhood and youth, nor did Evelyn or Marie Louise. In later years both sisters suffered from bouts of depression and were hospitalized on repeated occasions. Roger turned inward. He was extraordinarily shy and had no self-confidence. As a young man he tried his hand at various menial jobs—soda jerk, delivery man for a butcher—but a meaningful career seemed not to be in the cards. Perhaps that is why he was not married at twenty-seven and why he wanted to become a priest.

Roger had never told his family or friends about his secret desire. It took a long time for him to work up the courage, but, finally, he went to his priest and told him that he wanted to go to the seminary and prepare for the priesthood. Fifty-five years later, in his room in a nursing home, Roger still remembered the priest's response: "Roger, you would not make a good priest.

You are too scrupulous. You think everything is a sin. You would not be able to give your parishioners the grace they need. My suggestion to you," the priest said, "is to go get married."

That night Roger went to the novena, a devotional service dedicated to the Virgin Mary. If you "made a novena," that is if you went to church nine consecutive Tuesday nights, Mary would grant your petition or "intention." Roger did not tell anyone what his intention was. But at the novena at the Cathedral of St. John the Baptist Roger eyed a red-haired young woman whom he did not know personally, though he did know her family. Ethel Barnhill was from Cottonport, a small town fifty miles north of Lafayette. She was not yet twenty and was in Lafayette visiting her *nanaine*, what Catholics in non-Cajun cultures would call a godmother. Ethel was very close to Be'naine.

When the novena was over, Roger saw Ethel outside the church, and in an act that was completely out of character for him, called out, "Hey, Red, need a ride?" To his surprise, she said yes, and he drove her to Be'naine's house. On the way, his confidence building by the minute, Roger asked Ethel if she would like to go to the "picture show" with him. Again, she said yes.

Roger picked up Ethel the next night and they walked, maybe to give him more time for what he had planned, to the theater. On the way, twenty-four hours after they met, Roger asked Ethel to marry him! And she said, "I'll give you an answer on the way home after the movie." When the movie was over, as they walked home, she said, "Yes." The next day Ethel cancelled her engagement to a young man named James.

Roger asked Ethel to marry him because the priest told him that he was too scrupulous for the priesthood and that he should find himself a wife. Why did Ethel accept? To find security perhaps. Her father, Benjamin Swan Barnhill, died of a heart attack when he was twenty-five years old, and she was a child. One of her most vivid and painful memories from childhood was being forced to kiss the body of her father at the wake. It was the beginning of a fear of death that stayed with her all her days. She never attended another funeral the rest of her life, not even for her own mother.

Ethel's fear of death was exacerbated years later when she was sent to a boarding school near Cottonport. Because the family could not afford to pay her expenses, she was assigned chores to work off her tuition, room, and board. Her chores included cleaning the bedside "slop jars" belonging to the nuns. To get to the nuns' sleeping quarters—a large room with many beds—she had to walk down a hallway along the walls of which were large trunks containing the nuns' personal belongings. The other girls at the school circulated the rumor that the trunks were actually filled with the bodies of dead people. Ethel believed the story and held her hands on either side of her eyes, like blinders, as she walked down the hallway, trying not to see the forbidden and terrifying trunks. Her mother convinced the nuns to relieve Ethel of that chore, but the incident helped to create a necrophobia which reached exotic proportions in adult life.

Several years after the death of her beloved Benjamin, Henrietta Couvillion Barnhill married Charles Gremillion, who moved the young family from New Orleans back to the Couvillion home place near Cottonport, where Couvillions had lived for five generations, and where Ethel and her family lived in poverty.

Perhaps it was to find security that Ethel accepted Roger's proposal of marriage. Or perhaps it was to find safety. Ethel's stepfather, a slovenly man who weighed over 250 pounds, abused her sexually throughout her growing-up years. At first, Henrietta refused to believe Ethel's stories about Charles. But she must have had reason to suspect him, because one night after he had gone to bed, Henrietta sprinkled flour on the ground outside Ethel's bedroom window and on the sill. The next morning there were footprints in the white-powdered dirt and handprints on the window sill and flour on Charles's shoes and pants. Not long thereafter, Henrietta sent Ethel to the Catholic boarding school.

It was a dark family secret, one which no one talked about, not even Aunt Ruby, especially not Aunt Ruby, saintly Aunt Ruby, Ethel's only living sister. When I asked her about it, several years after Ethel died, Aunt Ruby told me that I should not have left the church and that I should have my marriage blessed. That is all she would say. When Aunt Ruby dies, Ethel's painful childhood secret will die with her.

Ethel and Roger—Mama and Daddy—were married on May 31, 1938, at St. Mary's Catholic Church in Cottonport. She was nineteen years old; he was twenty-seven. No two people were ever more ill suited for one another. They were incompatible for almost fifty years of marriage. Roger was passive and submissive in the extreme. Ethel was domineering and harsh, also in the extreme. Whatever feelings she had for him in the beginning quickly turned to disillusionment and disgust. She yelled at him, she taunted him, she badgered him, she ridiculed him. She humiliated him in front of the children; she humiliated him in front of anybody. Maybe it was an old anger which should have been aimed at Charles Gremillion, now long dead. Maybe she was punishing Roger for not being the tower of strength she needed to protect her. Maybe she was just mean. Roger never retaliated. He never even responded, except with the mousy frightened, foolish grin of the schoolyard runt who is always being pushed around by the neighborhood bully. The more Ethel abused him, the more he retreated inside himself; the more he retreated inside himself, the more she hated him for it. We were all afraid of Mama, but I think Daddy was afraid the most.

No Gray Lines On My Soul

My confirmation day was special because it was "my" day. In a family of ten children, the times when I had a day of my own, such as my birthday, were rare. My confirmation picture, taken in Grandma's yard, shows me standing proudly in my white dress, white veil, and white shoes, holding my rosary. The dress was Pookie's and it was too large for me—it kept slipping off one shoulder—but I stood proudly nonetheless.

In the confirmation ceremony we were given the name of a saint we could call on in times of temptation and stress. My confirmation name was Ruth. I wished the nuns had chosen a different name, because Ruth was the name of my youngest sister. Of course, I would never have said a word to the nuns about it, and I didn't. It meant, however, that I never asked St. Ruth to help me out of difficult situations as I asked, say, St. Anthony, St. Dymphna, or St. Theresa. These saints, one who was responsible for help with lost things, one who was the patron saint of the mentally ill, and one who was very close to Jesus, have stayed with me through the years.

The other special thing about confirmation was the admonition to be "soldiers of the cross." The bishop slapped each of us on the cheek to indicate that now we were strong enough to stand up for our religion in the face of adversity. I could not have known then that the first time my religion would be questioned, by a Bible-quoting Protestant college boy from north Louisiana, I would, after defending my faith as best I could, relinquish it and become a Southern Baptist. I never once thought of the slap in the face as a defense against proselytizers.

At about the time of my confirmation, I became obsessed with sin. I had learned about sin in catechism when I was taught the fundamentals of the faith in the ancient question and answer format:

Q: Who made you?
A: God made me.
Q: Why did God make you?
A: To love, serve, and obey him.

The nuns showed us pictures of the soul which they said was inside everyone. One picture showed a heart crisscrossed with ominous grayish-black lines. Under the picture was the caption: "The Unconverted Soul." On the next page there was a heart that was pure white with this caption: "The Converted Soul that is capable of loving, serving, and obeying God." I did not want to have an unconverted soul with grayish-black lines on it, so I tried with all my heart not to have sins of any kind on my soul—certainly not mortal sins which would send my soul straight to hell. Venial sins would not send my soul straight to hell, but I worked hard not to have them either.

Daddy encouraged us to go to confession every Saturday afternoon. Walking the several blocks to St. John the Baptist Cathedral, I would search my soul for a good sin to confess, but, as often as not, I would not be able to come up with a single sin worth feeling guilty about. Surely, I had committed a sin during the entire preceding week. You could bet that God would remember even if I could not.

The Lafayette Parish Court House was on the way to the cathedral where I intended to confess my sin, if I could think of one. Frustrated by my inability to dredge up a single noteworthy sin, I would sit on the grass of the court house and agonize over what to tell the priest. If I had wished that something bad would happen to somebody, that would be a sin. Or maybe I had told a little lie. But nothing came. Finally, feeling terribly guilty, I would get up and trudge to the cathedral and confess to the priest that I could not think of anything to confess. That was usually OK with him.

Grandma, pure and good Grandma, went to confession *at least* once each week. She did not have any sins to confess either, but I think she enjoyed confessing to nothing more than I did. Each week when she entered the confessional and said, "Bless me, Father, for I have sinned," the priest would recognize her voice and, irritated that she was about to waste his time, say: "Go to communion, Mrs. Bernard!" Grandma knew that she did not have anything to confess, but it pleased her that the priest would not hear her confession and she would come home and tell us all about it.

Grandma was more Catholic than the pope, Daddy liked to say. She was either at church, on her way to church, or on the way back from church. Church meant going to mass at St. John the Baptist Cathedral on Sundays and going to mass during the week at the nearby "colored" church. Actually, "colored people" were welcome in the cathedral—they sat in a section in the left rear—but the neighborhood church closest to where Grandma lived was attended mainly by black Catholics. So, that is where she attended mass during the week.

Grandma paid for Catholic schooling for me and my sisters. We attended a public school through the eighth grade, but when we were ready for high school, Grandma made sure that we went to Mt. Carmel. And she never let us forget it. "C'est moi qui paye," she would say. ("It is I who paid!") What would her life have meant if she had not taken it on herself to make sure her only son's children went to a Catholic school, what with his being married to an infidel!

Mama did not believe in God. She said she wanted to but couldn't. She did love St. Anthony, though. She would promise him money if he would find something she had lost; it was a sort of "finder's fee." Mama was always losing things, and occasionally she would find something she had lost, so St. Anthony did pretty well. Mama was conscientious about putting whatever money she had promised in the poor box at the church. She was convinced that if you did not pay St. Anthony what you owed after he had gone to the trouble of finding something for you, he would not be so willing to help you find the next thing you lost. Mama had great faith in St. Anthony. One day she told me that she could not see how people believe in God. I said, "Mama, you believe in God. His name is St. Anthony!"

My need to have sins to confess—If Jesus died for my sins, wasn't I duty bound to have some?—led to a peculiar preadolescent obsession. I convinced myself that any time and every time I touched something I was stealing, because in touching it I took away a few particles of it. Though I did not mean to steal, if I inadvertently took some of it with me, I was guilty of theft. When I sat on the ground and got up with a grass stain on my clothing, for example, I was convinced that I had stolen something from the grass and was, at last, guilty of a sin.

One day a friend and I were walking home from the municipal swimming pool. Choosing the shortest route, we walked across a complex of railroad tracks and decided to rest on the steps of the depot. When we got up, I noticed that I had a three- or four-inch smudge of oil on my leg. I knew that my concern for sin was unusual and that I had to hide it from my family and school friends. But I also knew that I had to make restitution. So, as we got up, I discreetly left a nickel on the step where I had "stolen" the grease and walked home with my friend.

Every night when we were little, Daddy would gather as many of us kids as he could find to say the rosary with him and the beautiful voices on the Radio Rosary of the Air. I never knew whether the program was produced locally or came from some broadcasting office of the Catholic church. My recollection is that it was professionally done, so I assume it was not a local production. A female voice would begin: "Hail, Mary, full of grace, the

Lord is with thee. Blessed art thou among women, and blessed is the fruit of thy womb, Jesus." A chorus would respond, "Holy Mary, Mother of God, forgive us our trespasses as we forgive those who trespass against us." (The nuns at Mt. Carmel told us that Protestants said, "Forgive us our debts as we forgive our debtors," and cautioned us that the Protestant version was not correct and that we should say "trespasses and those who trespass against us.") And Daddy expected us to respond with the chorus. Daddy was sincere and sweetly devout, but there was not a kid in the family who did not feel like a fool kneeling in front of the Philco console, talking back to the radio. So, as soon as word got around the house that it was almost time for the Radio Rosary of the Air, there was a stampede for the front or back door as we headed outside where Daddy could not catch us.

Friday was a very important day when I was in high school. That was the day that we Mt. Carmel girls got to go to mass at the cathedral and sit across the main aisle from the boys who attended Cathedral High School. We spent the entire hour alternately pretending not to notice one another and sending hand signals about when and where we would meet in the big gathering in front of the church at the conclusion of the mass.

Friday was also the day that we were forbidden to eat meat. Sometimes Mama made an oyster or shrimp gumbo; more often, though, it was couche-couche. When my oldest brother Phil worked in the oil fields in the years following high school, he would bring a fried-egg sandwich to work on Friday, as many of the roustabouts did. One day an old-timer got his calendar confused and brought a fried-egg sandwich for lunch on Thursday.

Phil asked, "What are you doing eating a fried-egg sandwich today?"

"Haven't you heard," the old man said sarcastically, "Catholics don't eat meat on Friday."

"I know," Phil said. "But today is Thursday." The old-timer

looked at his sandwich and realized that he would have to face another one just like it the next day.

"Well," he said, "I'm gonna make my Friday today." The next day he brought a ham sandwich.

All Fridays were important but Good Friday was special. The only problem was that observance of Good Friday was different for Daddy and for Mama. Very different! Daddy saw Good Friday as any good Catholic would: a day of solitude, prayer and participation in the Way of the Cross. Even though we attended public schools from kindergarten through the eighth grade, we were able to go to church with Daddy since Catholics were given permission to be absent without an excuse on Good Friday. Some of my brothers and sisters figured out that if they could talk Daddy out of going to church they could get a free day out of school, since the teachers had no way of knowing whether they actually went to the Way of the Cross. Phil and Jeannine and the others thought they were pretty smart getting out of school and not having to go to church, but Mama usually saw to it that they regretted their decision.

Mama's view of how to observe Good Friday was the opposite of Daddy's. She thought that of *all the days in the year* Good Friday was the one day God would want us to work! If Jesus had to suffer and die, the least we could do was to work hard that day so we could identify with his pain! It was downright unholy to spend time in church on Good Friday when Jesus had to suffer so. Mama did not care one whit about the religious aspects of Good Friday. She saw it as a chance to get a lot of work done around the house. Her "theology" was purely pragmatic.

Mama did all she could to get us not to go to church with Daddy. That put us kids in a bind. Not that we were torn between honoring our father or our mother. Rather, we were torn between going to the long, sad, boring Way of the Cross or staying home and letting Mama work us to death. Our only hope was that

Mama would decide to go somewhere and forget about how hard we had to work. She was so unpredictable that that was always a possibility.

One year I decided to stay home. That year Mama did not forget. First, she made us take everything out of all the kitchen cabinets, line them with shelf paper, and put everything back. Then she made us clean under the sink where roach droppings had become fossilized in the sticky remains of a spilled gallon of syrup. Within a week the shelf paper was torn to shreds, and the syrup had been spilled again.

The brothers and sisters who went to Good Friday services with Daddy returned taunting us, saying that they had made the better choice. We were not about to admit our mistake, so we taunted back, saying that they had to do all the kneeling, praying, crying, and being scared because the statues were covered with purple cloth and looked pretty spooky.

There was another special thing about Fridays. We believed that if a person went to mass and communion on the first Friday of each month for nine consecutive months, he or she would go to heaven on the first Friday after his or her death. So, if a person died on, say, Thursday, then the next day she or he would go to heaven, provided, of course, that she or he were free of mortal sin at the time of death. Older members of my extended family regularly went to the first Friday celebrations of the mass with every intention of completing the novena. My grandmother went to mass and communion every first Friday of her life, I think, and, if anyone was eligible to bypass purgatory, it was Grandma.

Grandma went to the funeral of virtually every person who died in Lafayette whether she knew them or not. It was her special ministry. Each day she would call the two funeral homes and ask the times of funerals scheduled that day. Then she would don her black overcoat which she wore every day no matter how hot and humid the south Louisiana weather was.

When Grandma arrived at the funeral home, she would kneel

beside the casket, say her rosary, and offer a prayer for the dead. Then she would extend condolences to the family, weep for the deceased, and take her place with the mourners on folding chairs in the viewing room. Then she would say her rosary again. After an appropriate period of time, Grandma would leave. On her way to the front door, she would approach a member of the funeral home staff and ask, "Who died, huh, cher?"

Grandma was so well known and so widely loved for this touching ministry that when she died at eighty-six, it seemed like the entire city of Lafayette attended her funeral. The Cathedral of St. John the Baptist was packed, and there were people who could not get in.

Stealing Dolls at the Church Fair

The church fair was not really a fair like the state fair, with a ferris wheel and a roller coaster and a sideshow with exotic animals, washed-up cowboy stars, and deformed people. It was an innocent, community money raiser for the Catholic church which we attended. The money was used to pay for the running of Catholic schools and the residences of the priests and nuns, which were always lavishly appointed and huge. I suppose it took a lot to pay for the nuns' and priests' upkeep—there were lots of fairs.

There were some things that you could always expect at the fair: handiwork of all sorts, crocheting, tatting, smocking, handmade scarves and tams, and samples of every kind of food Cajuns ate. Of course, there was gumbo. But there was also boudin. Boudin is vile! It is made with rice and the trash part of the pig stuffed into the casing of the small intestine with the intestine squeezed out to make room for the boudin. Boudin is spicy and greasy, but most people seemed to like it. Mama loved it. She never went to the church fair, but she always made us bring her some boudin.

Pookie, Donald, and I went to the fair for one purpose only: to take chances at the various booths in hope of winning a wonderful, glitzy prize. The tickets were typically a nickel or a dime or a quarter. The booth that attracted my attention was a game of chance that had as prizes beautiful handmade dolls. The faces of the dolls were miniscule, the hair was groomed and fluffy. There could be no finer dream to have come true than to go home with one of those fancy dolls in their fancy dresses and hairdos.

The way the game worked was that you put your money on a numbered block in a U-shaped table and the hawker spun a large wheel. If the wheel stopped on your number, you won one of those wonderful dolls. We played awhile, not winning anything, until we were just about out of quarters. Then it dawned on us that if we spread out, with Donald on one side of the U, me on another, and Pookie on the third side, we could wait until the wheel stopped and the hawker called out the winning number, then one of us could slip a quarter on the lucky square! We were so small and the game was packed with so many big people that no one was paying attention to us. It worked!

Time after time one of us had the winning number. And every time we won a gorgeous doll. Our "method" kept working until people began to look at one or another of us and say suspiciously, "You sure are lucky!" Finally, when we were either unable to carry all the dolls we "won" or we were out of quarters, we left.

Of course, Donald did not care about the dolls. So Pookie and I traded something for his share of our winnings. I do not remember what it was.

As Pookie and I walked home, loaded with the dolls and Mama's boudin, I knew and she knew that we didn't *really* win the dolls. Deep down we knew that we had done something wrong, but we felt that if we had not won them we had somehow earned them. In any case, the dolls were ours! And not even confession with its inevitable restitution was going to make us take them back!

The next thing was to figure out what to do with them. Things in our house never stayed where they were put. We had to find a place where they would be protected from the hands of the little ones. But it also had to be a place where Pookie and I could see and admire our dolls. That meant it had to be in the open and high. When we walked into the middle bedroom, our eyes went immediately to the statues of Jesus on the cross, Mary, and the Infant Jesus of Prague on the shelves in the corner, and we knew that was it! We would replace the statues of the saints with our new dolls. But we had to do it right away, because Daddy might come in and if he did he would take it personally, as if he were the one who had stolen the dolls. Daddy always thought everything was his fault. That's because Mama told him everything was his fault, and he believed her. Then he would ask us to say the rosary with him and try to make us feel sorry we had "won" the dolls and make us take them back. Hurriedly, we replaced Jesus on the cross, Mary, and the Infant Jesus of Prague statues with the dolls, putting the religious figures in the closet.

Oh, were the ladies beautiful! And, boy, did we feel guilty! But not right away.

The amazing thing is that Daddy never said a word. Either he did not notice the exchange or he noticed and let it go. Probably the latter, because he never fussed at us about anything without Mama's prompting, and Mama sure did not care about the statues, even if she noticed the dolls.

In time the dolls got dirtier and dirtier, and one day they were not there anymore. I never knew what happened to them. I suppose either one of the little ones made off with them or broke them or they became victims of one of Mama's periodic spells of house cleaning.

Ruby Falls

I spent summers with Aunt Lynn, Daddy's sister who lived in Broussard, a small village located about ten miles from Lafayette. Aunt Lynn loved me, and so did Uncle Voorhies. One day I got lost in Mongomery Ward when they were shopping. A store staff member found me and asked, "Who is your daddy?" I said, "Uncle Voorhies," which tickled both Uncle Voorhies and Aunt Lynn. This story was told so often over the years that I no longer know whether I remember getting lost or the story about getting lost. Aunt Lynn and Uncle Voorhies probably saved me from more hurts at home than I ever knew.

It was while I was on one of those wonderful summer excursions to Aunt Lynn's that I received a phone call from my older brother Phil telling me to come home immediately because our family was going on vacation. I could not believe my ears. A vacation? Our family? Yes, he said, and I needed to come home right then. The moment is vivid in my memory even now. The phone was on the dining room table. I was standing between the windows, receiver in hand, listening to a message I never dreamed I would hear.

"Our family go on a vacation? To Ruby Falls? What is Ruby Falls?"

Phil had no idea. But he was happy, and he said that I would be included and that we would leave within a day or two. It sounded like something Jane Wallace's family would do—not us Bernards. We were going on a vacation. I liked the way it sounded and had a wonderful feeling in my stomach. I was so proud. Aunt Lynn and Uncle Voorhies drove me to Lafayette.

Mama told us that ever since she was a little girl she had seen huge signs painted on the sides of barns inviting passersby to

"See Ruby Falls." She had made up her mind, she said, that one day she would do just that. The Standard Coffee Company, for which Daddy drove a route in a panel truck, selling coffee and a wide assortment of items from a catalogue, had given him one week off. That meant we had the weekend before, the five weekdays in between, and the weekend after for our first vacation ever. Nine days in all. And we were going to Ruby Falls. Whatever and wherever that was.

Within a couple of days the 1952 Buick Roadmaster, aqua and white with white sidewall tires, was loaded. The car was so big that we were able to place two full-sized trunks between the front and back seats. With the trunks, which were level with the back seat, we had the makings of a station wagon. It was a bed, a card table, seats for sightseeing, and wrestling mat. Mama made sure that we were well supplied with food to eat in the car—peanut butter and syrup, bread, powdered milk, and a can of Standard Coffee.

Early on Saturday morning we piled into the car, and off we went, Mama and Daddy, Phil, Jeannine, Pookie, Ruthie, Donald, Jamesy, Gordon, and me.

We were scarcely out of town when Mama said that we had to stop and visit one of her brothers, Gaston Gremillion, who lived in Opelousas. Gaston was the uncle who called each of us kids "Rosie," because he said it was too much trouble remembering all our names. While we were there, a friend of Uncle Gaston's dropped by and told us about Niagara Falls, from which he had just returned. He went on and on about how beautiful it was, how majestic and powerful the sound of water cascading to the earth. We listened in awe. But we thought, how could anything, even Niagara Falls, be better than Ruby Falls? Undaunted, Mama got us back into the car, and we headed north.

As we drove into towns we played "limousine." It was Phil's idea to pretend that our Buick was really a big limousine and that we were rich. When we entered the business district of a town, where we had to drive slowly and sometimes stop at traffic lights, Phil would arrange us kids in four rows of two to make it look as if we had four seats in back instead of one. Then he would order us not to move, no matter what.

"Just look straight ahead," he said, "kind of snotty like."

We drove through many small towns in Louisiana and Mississippi that way, looking straight ahead, stifling giggles, punching each other, and wondering "what all those people on the sidewalks must be thinking."

All along the way we saw signs like those Mama had described, signs that read, "See Ruby Falls." Typically, they were written in big capital letters on the side of the barn that sloped our way as we drove by. Each time we saw a "See Ruby Falls" sign we cheered and reminded ourselves of our good fortune. We did not stop—not to spend the night or to do much else—until we got to Tennessee.

At Ruby Falls we took an elevator to the bottom of the cavern, then followed a guide along a winding, well-worn path through scary rock formations for what seemed like forever. At one point, the guide turned off the lights, and we marveled over the suffocating darkness of the cave. He told us that the temperature in the cave was an eternal fifty-four degrees, as it was in every other cave in the world. Wow. This was really something.

Finally, we arrived at a modestly wide but tall opening in the cavern, where what I recall as a trickle of water was running down the wall to the floor of the cave. The guide was closest to the trickle; the curious vacationers, temporary spelunkers, faced the guide who now pointed to the water with his flashlight. After we had positioned ourselves to get a good look, the guide said slowly and proudly, over-enunciating each word: "See Ruby Falls."

There was a moment of silence, broken only by the oohs and aahs of the tourists. Then, to my dismay, Mama stepped out of the pack and asked the guide, "What did you say?"

He repeated, "See Ruby Falls."

Incredulous, Mama said, *"That's* Ruby Falls?"

Pleased with his role which allowed him yet another opportunity to pronounce those words which were painted on the sides of thousands of barns throughout the South, he said even more loudly, "Yes, Ma'am. That's Ruby Falls, all right."

Mama couldn't believe her ears or, more importantly, her eyes. She blurted out, her voice echoing off ancient rock formations, "Do you mean to tell me that dribble of water coming out of that hole in that rock up there is Ruby Falls?"

Again, the guide said, "Yes, ma'am," but this time with no fanfare, for by now he was beginning to suspect that this sightseer was not particulary pleased. Then Mama let it all out.

"I have seen signs on the sides of barns ever since I was a little girl that said, 'See Ruby Falls.' For as long as I can remember I have said to myself one day I will see Ruby Falls. I drove all the way from Lafayette, Louisiana, with my husband and eight children, without stopping, on the first vacation we have ever had. Oh boy, we thought, we are going to see Ruby Falls. And THAT'S Ruby Falls? That little bit of nothing? Well, we're going to Niagara Falls."

Mama turned on her heels and headed for the elevator, and it was all we could do to keep up with her.

Back in the Buick, settled atop the trunks and being very quiet for fear of Mama's embarrassment and anger, we began our trek north to Niagara Falls by way of Cincinnati where in the wee hours of the morning Mama was stopped for speeding. Awakened from our sleep by the sound of a siren and the sight of a flashing light, we kids were scared out of our wits as we watched Mama get out of the car to talk with the officer.

After a few minutes Mama got back in the driver's seat and said smugly, "He tried to give me a ticket. But I flirted with him a few minutes and told him how we had been disappointed at Ruby Falls and were on our way to Niagara Falls and with so many children to feed, could he please excuse us from getting a speeding ticket, and he did." She was obviously very pleased with her performance, and I was proud of our Godlike-in-omnipotence Mama.

Niagara Falls was everything Mama had promised us it would be. It was ten thousand Ruby Fallses, and not only that, we did not have to walk miles through a dank, dark underground cavern to get to it. Mama made us stand by the railing and look and look and look, until we begged her to let us stop standing there because we were tired and soaked to the skin.

"Just keep looking," she said, "until you can't look anymore."

Mama told us how Niagara Falls generated electricity for people to use in their homes and how important it was to industry. Mama was smart. She knew about such things. I think Daddy knew a lot, too. But around Mama he was like one of the kids. He did what we did; he saw what Ethel told him to see.

Then, abruptly, Mama said that we needed to go because once you have seen Niagara Falls it is just more of the same. That was vintage Mama. Once she got to the heart of a thing, it was time to move on. Even with all the looking, it did not take us very long to "see Niagara Falls;" it took about as long as it took us to "see Ruby Falls."

We got the same quick look at Lake Erie. Mama insisted that we take a swim. "Go ahead," she said. "Even if you don't swim more than a minute. Then, you can tell your friends that you swam in Lake Erie. You will never forget it, and you will always have something to impress your friends with."

Then, Mama told us that we were so close, it would be a shame to come all that way and not "see Canada." Going to Canada would be special, she said, because that is where our Acadian ancestors came from. Never mind that Nova Scotia was hundreds of miles away.

In the thirty minutes or so we were in Canada, we bought some gingerbread and some postcards—gingerbread to eat and postcards to prove to our friends back home that we had actually been to Canada. It was during our brief stay north of the border that Mama had the idea that since we were so close we might as well go home by way of New York City. "Ever since I was a little girl," she said, "I have wanted to see New York City." Mama was unpredictable and extravagant, but to a child on her first vacation she was great fun.

By now we kids were used to being told to see this, see that, let's go see if this is worth seeing. Mama called all the shots all of our lives, but it was most noticeable on our trip, because there was nothing, like school or church or chores, to cushion her freewheeling style. She was on a roll with the nonstop decision making.

Somewhere, as we were driving up and down the Catskill Mountains, Mama got stopped for speeding again. But this was not dark Cincinnati in the wee hours of the morning where she could flirt with a policeman and talk him out of giving her a ticket. This was broad daylight, and this highway patrolman was serious.

Mama had been having a good time and had been leading all of us in having a good time, too. As we went up a hill, she would yell out, "Here we go up." Then, as we topped the hill and headed down, she would say, "Whee! Here we go down." Then, "Here comes another one." In the back seat, we eight kids were having the time of our lives, making so much noise that only a siren could be heard above the din.

"Ma'am, you were going eighty-nine miles an hour in a fifty-five-mile-per-hour zone," the officer said. "But that's not the worst part. Are all those your children?" he asked, pointing to the tangle of wide-eyed kids holding on to one another in the back seat. "I don't have a place in my book to check off 'endangering the lives of children'," he said, "but if I did I would."

Mama did not act smart this time. She did not even try to

flirt with him. Then the policeman announced solemnly that he was going to have to take us in, just like they said on TV. I was *so* scared. We were all scared.

No one said a word as we obeyed the officer's instruction to follow him thirty-five or forty miles down the highway, then off the highway on to a country road until we arrived at a large white house with huge trees in front. The officer drove real slow all the way and kept his blue light on, but at least he turned off the siren.

Mama said that she and Daddy would both have to go see about the ticket and for us to stay real still and not make trouble while they were gone. My mind began to race. Would they put Mama and Daddy in jail? Would we have to go to jail, too? Mama seemed scared and nervous. That made me scared and nervous. We always felt what Mama felt. When she was happy, we were happy. When she was worried, we were worried. Of course, when she was angry, we were scared. But, mostly, we felt what she felt.

Jeannine and Phil only made my anxieties worse. After Mama and Daddy left, they began telling stories to us little ones about how we would never see Mama and Daddy again. They said there was no telling what the "law" would do to Mama since she had been caught speeding twice since we left Lafayette. They said there was some kind of network that lets police officers in every state know who the troublemakers are on the highway.

"They let Mama go in Cincinnati," Phil said, "but this time they are going to throw the book at her, and we had better be real good when she comes back because you can bet your life she will be in a bad mood."

Mama had parked the car on the road next to a barn. Inside the barn we could see a conveyor belt with bales of hay being carried up into the loft. For a while I watched the bales, fixing my eye on one bale until it reached the top and went out of sight, and then fixing on another bale, just trying to keep my mind occupied, all the while feeling scared that something really bad was going to happen to us. For a while, none of us said anything. Then, Phil and Jeannine told us that the conveyor belt had bales of hay on it now, but just wait.

"When the police get through with Mama and Daddy, they will take them somewhere far away and lock them up," they said, "because it is not right to speed. Then the police will not know what do do with us kids, so they will strap us to that conveyor belt, and we will go up just like the bales of hay, except when *we* get to the top, there will be a slicing machine, like the one at Benoit's Grocery Store back home where we buy baloney. You know the machine at Benoit's?" Phil asked. "Well," he said, "the machine at the top of the conveyor belt is bigger and sharper and will slice us faster than baloney."

Pookie, Donald, Jamesy, Gordon, Ruthie, and I—all six of us—started to cry. Jeannine and Phil never cracked a smile. They just let us cry and cry and cry. Then, when they saw Mama and Daddy walking toward the car they said, "You kids be quiet. We are just kidding. Here come Mama and Daddy. Stop crying. Mama and Daddy are having enough trouble without hearing all of y'all crying." With great effort we stifled our tears and sobs, either because we really did not want to cause Mama and Daddy more trouble or because we did not want to admit that we had been taken in by Phil and Jeannine.

When Mama and Daddy got to the car, we were anxious to find out what happened. Of course, Daddy did not say anything. Mama said that she told the officer about how we were all from Louisiana where everything is flat and how we were having such a good time riding up and down the hills, like a roller coaster, she said, that we just forgot all about how fast we were going. All of which was true, of course. She said that she had to pay some money, but that we were going on to New York anyway.

Mama was a little less carefree than she had been before. Being stopped twice for speeding on one trip must have gotten to her. She did not laugh and try to make us feel that we were so smart to be on this trip. She just drove and was real quiet for a long time. Daddy was real quiet as usual. We were real quiet, too. My fear had abated somewhat, but I had a sick feeling in my stomach like I was going to throw up.

Years later I found out that the ticket cost Mama $25 and that gasoline for the trip cost $80. Since Mama and Daddy had only $150 for the entire trip, the ticket was a serious blow. Maybe that is why, when we got to New York City in the middle of the night, we did not bother to look for a place to stay.

Mama woke us up at three o'clock and said, pointing into the foggy distance, "See that light out there? That is the Statue of Liberty. Now, you can go back and tell all your friends that you saw the Statue of Liberty." Then, she explained to us how the French had given the money for the construction of the statue and that we were French, too, and that we should be proud. I can still see that dim light in the harbor and Mama pointing and making sure that we got a good look, as good as we could get considering that there really was not much to see.

By four-thirty in the morning Mama had found the Empire State Building. It was another of her "ever since I was a little girl" dreams. The only thing I remember about the Empire State Building is that while we were straining our necks trying to see through the fog to the light on top, Gordon peed on the sidewalk.

That is about all we saw of New York City—dim lights in the fog. Except for the only other place in New York City that Mama had always wanted to see since she was a little girl. It was just breaking day when we drove through the Bowery. Mama drove slowly so she could tell us about all the famous alcoholics who ended up lying on the sidewalk dead drunk. We eyed the pathetic men carefully, our windows rolled up and doors locked for fear that they might come get us.

Our route homeward took us through Washington, D.C., and we saw all the sights in the nation's capitol: "There is the Washington Monument.... That is the Library of Congress....

You can tell your friends that you saw the White House." We did not stop once in Washington, not even to let Gordon pee on some famous sidewalk.

The lack of money explains why, on our entire vacation—from Lafayette to Ruby Falls to Niagara Falls, across to Canada, down to New York City and south to Washington, then down the east coast through the Shenandoah Valley for a swim in the Gulf of Mexico at Panama City, a total of almost 3,500 miles—we stopped for a grand total of two nights. All the rest of the time—nine days in all—we drove, averaging almost 400 miles a day. Actually, Mama did all the driving. As a child Daddy had encephalitis, which is why, it was explained to us, he would fall asleep without even going through the drowsy stage. So, he slept most of the way across the country. Only things like police sirens could wake him.

On the last night of our vacation we drove straight through to Lafayette from Panama City, pulling into our driveway at 326 General Mouton at about eight o'clock Monday morning—just in time for poor Daddy to get his truck loaded and go on his route.

In later years, after most of us were gone, Mama became something of a world traveler, making every World's Fair she could. But the trip to Ruby Falls was our very first family vacation. And our last. Within a few years, Phil, Jeannine, and Pookie, though still in their teens, would leave home. And three years after that, I would leave, too, as we learned, each in our turn, that all was not as it seemed to our young, believing eyes. Still, even now, forty years later, knowing what I know, recollections of Mama's first vacation bring a smile to my face and a warm glow to my heart.

Chocolate Mush
and Biscuits

I remember as a child driving with my family at night, seeing houses with the glow of lights in the windows and letting my imagination go where it willed. Selecting a house on my side of the car, I would look at it long and hard and think, "I bet the people who live in that house are happy." I would not think that about every house we passed that had lights on in the window, only about particularly "cozy" houses that looked like the ones in "Father Knows Best."

I imagined that inside the house there would be a happy mother and a happy father who loved their children and did not fuss at them or ask them to do things they did not know how to do. It would be a house that I could bring my friends to and not worry that it would be dirty and strewn with clutter, and there would be food in the cabinets (I did not know the word "pantry" while growing up) and no roaches in the refrigerator. It would have pictures on the wall and fluffy bedspreads, soap in the bathroom, toilet paper on the roll, and knickknacks that were not broken on shelves that fit in the corner of the room. It would have a lock on the door, and I would have a key. It would have closets that had shelves, and you could find what you were looking for. It would have a clothesline that did not sag when you hung the clothes, and there would be enough pins to hang all the clothes that needed hanging. It would be in a neighborhood where people cared about you and did not gossip. The houses with lights in the window would be home to people whose houses and yards and lives were decent, and who would invite you to come in without having to clean up first, and they would let children play in their yard.

For as long as I could remember I wanted to have friends over after school or maybe even overnight, but our house and yard were an embarrassment to me.

At one time when I was in elementary school, there was a dilapidated trailer house in our front yard. It embarrassed Grandma. "I am not proud," she said, "but I would not have that in my yard." One day Mr. Godfrey, the band director, gave me a ride home after practice. En route I remembered the trailer house and Grandma's injured pride. So, I gave Mr. Godfrey directions to Grandma's, as though it were my house. After he drove off and I could no longer see his dark green Chevrolet, I walked home. I did not even go in and say hello to Grandma. I was too embarrassed.

Our yard had no grass, no flowers, no bushes, no vegetation whatever, except in the summer when a vine sprang up, from I don't know where, magic I supposed, and covered the screened-in front porch where we had rockers and a swing. In the summer we used the porch as a respectable "room." Later, when I was a teenager, the vine gave us privacy and sometimes I would invite a date to sit on the swing. One spring Pookie and I planted zinnias on either side of the sidewalk. When they bloomed we were so, so proud. Our yard looked like yard of the month.

Once—only once—I invited two friends, Jane Wallace and Martha Tolson, to have a slumber party at my house. Jane and Martha were the first friends who invited me into their houses. My other friends were "outside" friends, which meant that we played on the sidewalk or on the street and not in each other's houses.

Jane was my "big deal" friend. Her father was a Presbyterian minister. Jane had long, straight, thick blonde hair which she wore in a low-gathered ponytail, and big blue eyes, and blonde hair on her arms and legs. The hair is what I remember most.

People in my family had lots of black hair on their arms and legs. I was embarrassed by my hair and tried to hide it when we played circle games or climbed trees or did anything which might show my legs. I felt very different when I was with my friends. I was the only one with all that dark hair on her arms.

Jane was so pretty. She looked like one of the dolls I saw in stores. There was no Cajun in Jane. None at all. What a life I would have, I often thought, if I could be like Jane Wallace.

Martha Tolson was a year younger than Jane and me, but she was my friend, and I used to play canasta at her house every afternoon in the summer. I was very envious of Martha's family. There was a mother, a father, a daughter, and a son. That's all. There weren't a lot of extra people around to be in the bathroom when you needed to go or to take a bath. Each person in the family had her or his own toothbrush. Martha had a room of her own. The Tolsons lived upstairs in a duplex. To me, rich people lived upstairs, no matter that it was the top floor of an apartment.

There was one feature of Martha's family life that I could not believe could be so consistent and feel so good to me. Each afternoon, they would set the table for dinner that evening, with a tablecloth, four plates (turned over), silverware, and glasses in place. Every day. Every day! Not one afternoon was the table not set for the evening meal.

There is no way my family would have done that. In the first place, we would not have had a tablecloth or dishes to match. And we would never have had the consistency to do something—anything—the same way day after day after day. When it was Martha's turn to set the table, her mother would call, "Martha, it is time to set the table for dinner. (Dinner? We only had supper.) Please tell your friends 'bye for now." It was so pleasant. What a dream.

The only bad thing about visiting Jane or Martha at their homes was that sometimes I would get a scared feeling when I left, like I was leaving something behind. I do not know why I felt that, but I did. Maybe that was the first inkling I had that my family was not like other families. It had never occurred to me that there might be people who were not on TV who really lived like that.

On the night of my slumber party, everything was going well in the one room which I had cleaned until about midnight when one of my friends said, "What do we get for a midnight snack?"

I had not thought about that. In our family we were lucky to have supper, much less a midnight snack. We never had extra food to snack on. And I knew the roaches in the kitchen would be embarrassing. Suddenly, I regretted that I had invited Jane and Martha. Thinking quickly, I told my friends, "Stay here, and I will get you a snack."

"We'll help you," they said.

"No," I said with finality. "I want to surprise you. Besides, I can fix the snack a lot better if you stay here and let me do it myself. I will get all mixed up if you are with me in the kitchen." This satisfied my friends, and they stayed in the assigned bedroom.

The kitchen and the bedroom where we were having the slumber party were adjacent. As I turned the knob to go into the kitchen, I warned my friends again that I would be unhappy if they were to come in and help me; I wanted to *surprise* them. With fear and trembling, I opened the door to the kitchen, quickly slipped through the tiny opening I had made, flipped the switch and the light in the ceiling came on. That was not to be taken for granted, for many times the only working light in the kitchen was the small fluorescent bulb on the backsplash of the electric stove. Luckily, this night the light in the ceiling came on, and I began trying to figure out what I would do for a "snack."

In the fourth grade I had taken home ec, which is where I learned to make biscuits from scratch. My daddy loved my biscuits; he wanted me to make them every day. I fussed and fussed and ended up making biscuits about once or twice a week, hating all the while that I had ever learned. But now it occurred to me that those biscuits would save me. I could make biscuits for my friends. But I had cooked for ten people for so long that I did not have a good sense of the amount of food people eat, and the only recipe for biscuits was enough for fifteeen or so people. So I followed my recipe and made enough biscuits for an army. Even then I feared that the pans of biscuits might not be enough food, so I made some french fries as well.

But what in the world would Jane and Martha drink? My family did not drink when we ate. I do not believe we ever drank anything, except Mama and Daddy drank coffee. Surely, I drank water, but I do not remember it. We never had enough glasses for all of us anyway, and the ones we had were always dirty. But I had noticed in the school cafeteria that most people drank with their meals, and I knew that I should have something for my two waiting slumber-party friends to drink. Grandma came to my rescue. Or more exactly, Grandma's hot chocolate.

When I say "Grandma," I mean my father's mother, Irma Landry Bernard, called "Soeur" (Sister) by everyone because she was so widely loved. My mother's mother, Henrietta Gremillion, lived only two blocks from our house on General Mouton, but I have only the vaguest memories of visiting her. I do not recall that she ever visited us. I can only assume that the wall between Mama and her mother was so thick and unclimbable that we children never got to know our maternal grandmother the way we got to know Daddy's mother. I can only imagine what the issues were.

Whenever I was hungry I could always walk the short blocks to Grandma's house and ask her to make some "chocolate mush." She would usually be crocheting, sitting in her cane-back rocker, which had long since stretched to fit her humpback. She was a one-person factory. She crocheted scarves of all sizes, bedspreads, booties, rosary purses, and tams, the scarf-like head coverings we wore to mass. But she would immediately stop crocheting, go to the kitchen, make chocolate milk with Hershey's cocoa, warm it and put bread in it. I could eat four pieces of bread in one bowl. Every time she made chocolate mush, she would check to be sure I really wanted four pieces of bread.

"I never ate more than one piece of bread at a time in my whole life," she would say, intimating that I could not possibly want four pieces of bread. But in the end, she would put the bread in the warm chocolate milk, and it always tasted so good.

I found the Hershey's cocoa, mixed the appropriate amount in water, then added some Pet milk so the drink would be richer and less lumpy, and my midnight snack was ready.

Jane and Martha could not believe what I had done. They were amazed that I could make scratch biscuits, french fries, and hot chocolate. They went on and on about it. I was surprised that they were surprised. In fact, I was embarrassed. I began to worry that maybe it wasn't "normal" for me to know how to do all that. Jane did not know how to make biscuits. Martha could not make french fries. Why not? Because their mothers cooked for their families. I knew how because I had to know how. Why? Because Mama did not or would not cook for us. Even my crowning achievement was a source of uncertainty, discomfort, and embarrassment.

Still, I felt proud that I had solved the problem of the midnight snack and that my friends liked what I made. For weeks afterward, they told other friends at school that Rosie could actually cook. I felt good about that. But I never had friends over again.

A Dollar for Your Little Girl

I grew up thinking "Jew" was a verb. Not that I knew what a verb was. But I knew less about Jews than I did about verbs. Growing up in south Louisiana in the late forties and fifties, it never occurred to me that there was anyone who was not Catholic. It was like girls were built like girls and boys were built like boys, and what we all had in common were mothers and fathers, brothers and sisters, and we were all Catholics. One day I got into an argument with Joan Must, a friend from elementary school. Joan was a Protestant, the only one I knew at the time—well, the only one I knew I knew—and she said that Jesus was a Jew. I said that Jesus was a Catholic. Besides Joan, everyone in my world was Catholic. In pre-Oil Boom days in Lafayette, Catholic is what we were before we were Americans or Cajuns. Maybe not before we were Cajuns, because being Cajun and being Catholic were the same thing.

Mama shopped for clothes for the ten of us at a store in Breaux Bridge which she called "the Jew." I did not especially like to go to "the Jew." I suppose it was because I really had no part in what always turned out to be a shopping frenzy. Mama made all of the decisions, of course, which is why it always turned out to be a frenzy.

"Here, do you want this, Rosie? Pookie, will this fit? Better take ten of those—hell, I'll take the case."

Mama loved to go to "the Jew." And she only went when she felt good. Or maybe going made her feel good. Mama liked doing things that got her hyped up, because they brought life to her. "Raise hell," she used to say, "it will make you more interesting."

The thing Mama liked most about the "Jew" was the bargaining. She would go through the store piling up clothes she wanted to buy. When her pile was high enough to suit her, she would go to the register and immediately start haggling over the price. The "Jew"—Heymann Cohen—would give Mama a price. Of course, that would not be *the* price. Mama would then give him a song and dance about having ten kids and a husband with a fledgling Standard Coffee business. Mr. Cohen had heard about Daddy's ineptness for more years than he cared to remember. But it was a game they played, with unspoken rules, and as a girl I could not say who was the winner.

One of the unspoken rules was that the haggling only went so far. Mama would do all she could to "Jew" Mr. Cohen down, but at some point the bargaining would stop, because both parties knew that the price on the table really was the price. Only once did Mama go beyond that point. One day, for reasons known only to her, she kept haggling without the expected grace to stop at the appropriate price. Mr. Cohen allowed the dickering to go back and forth several more times, then he exploded in anger and frustration.

"OK, Mrs. Bernard," he said. "You can have the clothes for that price. Take the things and go. Oh, by the way," he said, as we gleefully gathered up the bundles, "here's a dollar for your little girl."

Mama did not know what to make of this unexpected gift, but she knew that somehow she was supposed to be insulted. So, indignantly, she swooped up her "bargain" and stalked out.

This incident with Heymann Cohen and the time that Joan Must told me that Jesus was a Jew were all I knew about Jews growing up.

Mrs. Dupuis

In 1988, when I was an administrator at a Quaker college in North Carolina, Jeannine, Pookie, Ruthie, and I met at a hotel in Houston for a two-day catching-up session. We were all grown up now with families of our own. It had been several years since we had been together. Pookie was in the States for an extended visit, and it is only a three-hour drive from Lafayette to Houston, where I was attending a conference, so she and the others met me when my meeting was over. For two days the four of us relived our lives, shared our accomplishments and our failures, talked, laughed, cried, smoked, and drank a lot.

On our first night together, someone, I do not remember who it was, mentioned Mrs. Dupuis. It had been more than thirty years since I had last thought about Mama's friend, the one whose little boy had a clubfoot. When I was a girl and my older brother and sisters were still home, Mama would announce a couple of times each week, "I am going to Mrs. Dupuis." I have no memory of ever asking who Mrs. Dupuis was or if I could go, too. When Mama went to visit Mrs. Dupuis, she just went, that's all. Like we went out to play, or went to Grandma's, except we would not have told Mama where we were going.

Once Mama told us, "I am going to New Orleans with Mrs. Dupuis. Her little boy has a clubfoot and needs an operation. It has to be done in New Orleans. She needs me. I will be gone several days, probably three or four."

Oh, I thought. It was a little out of the ordinary, but it never occurred to me to question her. Mama left and was gone for almost a week. When she came back, I asked, "How is Mrs. Dupuis's little boy?"

"What?" she said. "He's OK." That was all there was to that.

"What ever happened to Mrs. Dupuis?" I now asked my sisters.

Jeannine and Pookie looked at me as though they could not believe what I was saying. "Rosie," Jeannine said, "don't tell me you don't know."

"Know what?"

"There was no Mrs. Dupuis."

"No Mrs. Dupuis? What are you talking about? Mama went to see her all the time and we stayed home and cleaned the house and she had a little boy with a clubfoot."

Jeannine and Pookie were incredulous. "There was no Mrs. Dupuis, Rosie. It was a cover. When Mama wanted to be with one of her lovers, she said she was going to see Mrs. Dupuis."

I could not believe what I was hearing. Jeannine knew and Pookie knew. Ruthie, the youngest, and I did not know. But Pookie was only thirteen months older than I. How could she know and I not know? What was wrong with me that I did not see what they saw?

"How long have you known?" I asked.

"Since we were kids," they said.

"Why didn't you tell me?"

"It never occurred to us that you didn't know. Everybody knew."

"She lied to us?" I asked.

"That was the least of what she did to us!"

"Are you sure?"

"Of course, Rosie. There was no Mrs. Dupuis."

I do not know why I found it so hard to believe that Mama would have affairs outside the house. I had known for many years about her affairs *in* our house. That is why I ran away at fourteen and never went back. Why should I be surprised that she met men elsewhere?

I do not know when the affairs started. Nor do I know why they started. I know that Mama was bitter about the way her life had turned out and frustrated with Daddy and angry and, I learned in the years after I left home, possessed by very powerful drives.

I suppose one clue as to when the affairs started was when Mama had locks put on the outside doors. The doors had not always had locks. Mama had said that it was too easy to lose the key, and we would not be able to get in when she was not home. But one day she had locks put in.

From that day on, the first child home from school became Mama's unwilling sentry. It was his or her responsibility to pass on to the next child home the message, "The door is locked." There was always something ominous about it—"The door is locked"—and it was always whispered. The word would be passed on as one brother or sister after another arrived in the front yard and saw the others at the side of the house where we had a swing hung from the limb of a tree. The word hardly needed to get around. We knew the door was locked; why else would they be outside playing? Even so, somebody would say, "The door is locked," and the word would be passed on.

At first we didn't know why the door was locked. We just knew something was not right. And we knew we had better not rattle the door or Mama would get angry and whip us later. Mrs. Landry, who rented from the Toneys, used to tell us, "Your mother leaves you outside to roost like chickens."

Sex had always been a topic of open conversation around our house, especially among Mama, Jeannine, and Pookie. Still, I was late learning about sex. Once they were talking about a boy Jeannine was dating. Mama said that he was so naive that he wouldn't know where to "put it." I did not know what she was talking about. Another time, Jeannine and Pookie told me that Mama said the young college men she dated liked her because they said she was "tight." I did not know what that meant either; but I knew it had to do with sex.

Aunt Lynn, with whom I spent summer vacations, was

obsessed with sin—her sin, my sin, anyone's sin. She was especially uncomfortable with sex. "Don't put your hand in that special place," she would tell me. She said that I could touch it when I washed it, but that should be done only once a day and very quickly. She also said that the Blessed Virgin cries every time she sees girls do "that." Mama said that was foolishness and that Aunt Lynn was scrupulous. I did not know what scrupulous meant, nor could I figure out why Aunt Lynn did not want me to put my hand in the "special place." I asked Sister Marie Therese, and she said I should forget it.

Needless to say, Mama and Daddy slept in separate bedrooms; the less Mama had to do with Daddy, the better it suited her. So when he wanted to have sex, he would go to Mama's room. But we lived in a small house. Ten of us, eight children and our parents, lived in three bedrooms and shared one bathroom. Nothing that happened anywhere in the house could be kept secret. When anyone was glad or sad or hurting, we all knew it. We may not have talked about it, in fact, we did not talk about it, but we knew. So, we all knew when Mama and Daddy were having sex. We could hear everything. Mama would act very disgusted about the whole thing. We could hear her say, "If you are going to do it, do it." Then, "Push, Roger, push." And then, "Now get out of here."

Mama told us that Daddy was incompetent at sex, that he prayed as he "did it" and that he couldn't "leave it in." She said, "Roger was finished in two minutes. Julio and I did it all night." She once bragged that with Julio she came ten times in one night. Mama told us that Daddy always took off his scapular first.

The only time Mama insisted on having sex with Daddy was when she knew she was pregnant by one of her lovers. Mama liked "Latins." She said they were smart, rich, and sexy. Mama wanted us to like Latin boys. Pookie dated and married John Gonzales who was from Venezuela. I dated a Latin boy once. He got fresh with me in the movie theater, and I felt very guilty.

After the movie, we went back to Grandma's and sat in the living room. He gave me a sterling silver bracelet as a gift, but I felt so bad about what I had let him do to me that I screamed, "I don't want that," and threw it into the fireplace. A few days later I made a modest but futile attempt to retrieve the bracelet. I was relieved when I could not find it in the ashes.

Some of Mama's lovers, like Edward and Julio, were "Latins." Others, like Mason and "old, skinny, hunchback" Sanders, who stole drill bits from oil-field equipment companies in Oklahoma and sold them in south Louisiana, were not. Mason was a farmer Mama met in the cane fields near Youngsville. Three of my brothers and sisters were fathered by Mama's lovers. The rest of us talked in hushed tones about the ones who didn't "belong" to Daddy. Mama bragged about it. In her later years she would go to Jeannine's every day and drink. "Liquor makes me forget," she said, "and I think of something else besides the pain." That is when she told Jeannine unashamedly, "I threw down the diaphragm when I was with Mason and said to him. 'I want to have one child who is not crazy like Roger.'" She did.

Jeannine, poor Jeannine, was old enough to know what was going on and has suffered more than the rest of us. When she was twelve Mama made her responsible for handling telephone calls from her lovers. It was Jeannine's job to make sure that they did not find out about one another. All Mama's lovers knew Jeannine by name, even before she was a teenager.

Jeannine told me, "Only God and I knew. I never told anyone." The truth is that everybody knew. Members of our extended family knew. The neighbors knew. The mother of Nancy DeBlanc, Jeannine's best friend knew. Mrs. DeBlanc did not want her daughter to be seen with the daughter of Ethel Bernard, so she would not let Nancy walk home from school with Jeannine. The girls remained friends, however. They would walk together until they got close to home. Then they would separate before Nancy's mother saw them.

One time I saw Mama having sex with Julio. They were on the bed in the back room; he was in his shorts. I was frightened, embarrassed, and confused. I felt like I had committed the worst sin in the world and wanted to go to confession right then. But there was no time for that. So I ran outside and hid under the house, all the way in the middle where the fern was thick so no one could get me. Mama and Julio must have realized that I had seen them, because they came out and knelt beside the house, peering underneath, calling, "Come on out."

"You didn't see anything," they said. "See, here we are. There's nothing wrong. Come on out. Everything's OK."

I sat very still and did not say a word. After a while, they gave up and went back into the house. I do not recall if Mama ever spoke to me about the incident.

So, why, after all I had seen in that house, after all the humiliation and pain I had suffered because of Mama, why was I shocked to learn that there was no Mrs. Dupuis? Could it be that in spite of everything—in spite of everything—I still had a need to trust Mama? Could it be that there was still something within me that could be betrayed? Could she still hurt me even from the grave, years after I swore that she would never hurt me again?

No Mrs. Dupuis. It hurts even today.

How the Day Goes

The pounding would not stop. It would not. No matter how far I pressed my head into the pillow, it would not stop. Poor Aunt Lynn. I was staying at her house, sleeping on the day bed she had fixed for me in the dining room, when it started. And she did not know what to do.

Even in the calmest circumstances, there was a nervousness about Aunt Lynn that made me uncomfortable. Her voice was always thin and had a trembly, tentative quality about it, and her brow seemed permanently wrinkled. Having been hospitalized at Pineville more than once for what was known generically as a "nervous breakdown," Aunt Lynn had the look of a victim about her. You knew that she had been a victim and that she feared that she would be again. "Poor Evelyn," people used to say, "she's too good."

It was not a headache. It was—a pounding. As though someone were inside, beating on the inside of my skull—thud! thud! thud!—shouting, "Let me out of here. Can you hear me? Can anyone hear me? I want to get out." It frightened me, partly because I did not understand what was happening inside my own body and partly because if the pounding did not stop, Aunt Lynn would have to send me home.

I do not know why I had been singled out to be the one of the ten who could go to Aunt Lynn's. But the weeks I spent with Aunt Lynn and funny, cynical Uncle Voorhies were the highlights of my hot, steamy summers. Aunt Lynn's house, painted a glistening white-white with black-green shutters, sat on a maze of brick pillars three or four feet tall, a precaution against flooding. Geraldine Girouard and I played under the house when it was dry.

Uncle Voorhies drove an ambulance for the Charity Hospital in Lafayette, and every once in a while he would have to take a patient to the Charity Hospital in New Orleans, which was bigger and offered more services. He always took Aunt Lynn and me along for the ride. Aunt Lynn insisted on sitting in the middle between Uncle Voorhies and me. It was years later before I found out why.

I liked going to Aunt Lynn's. She and Uncle Voorhies liked me. I had all the food I wanted and someone who was sweet to me all the time. That is why I wanted the pounding to stop—so I could stay at Aunt Lynn's. Or so I would not have to go home.

At first I tried to ignore it. Then I tried to get involved in something I liked to do, like reading. But nothing could make the pounding inside my head stop. Finally, I went to bed, put my pillow over my head, and prayed the "Hail Mary" over and over and over. But the Blessed Virgin ignored my plea.

I was in bed when I overheard Aunt Lynn and Uncle Voorhies talking in the kitchen. "Vo'," she said in her worried voice, "we have to take Rosie home. I don't know what else to do." So, they put me in the car and drove me back to Lafayette.

Someone had already cleared the stuff off the bed in the middle bedroom by the time I got there. The ceiling fan in the kitchen was on, as it was all summer. The whirring of the blades was both a comfort and a pain to me. The continuous drone of the fan was like an anesthetic for me. Lying in bed, I focused my gaze on a spot on the ceiling and hummed, trying to match the pitch of the motor in the next room. This conscious attempt at self-deception would have worked more effectively if the revolution of the blades had not been in perfect synchronization with the pounding that would not stop.

I do not know how long I lay in bed before Mama came home. Nor do I know where she had been. What I know is that Mama cared about whatever my problem was. That was not to be assumed. Mama had a simple theory on childhood maladies:

don't deal with any complaint unless the ailment had been around for several days or it was bleeding or had been caused by a rusty nail. Her routine response to any complaint was to say that she had it, too—regardless of the malady. If Donald complained of a headache, she would say, "I have a headache, too." If James said that the blisters on his feet hurt, Mama said that the blisters on her feet hurt, too. I suppose that with ten children she could not get into pampering any of us. Where would it stop? And there was a practical wisdom to her approach: sooner or later we always got well. Our sores always healed, and our headaches always went away.

Mama leaned over my bed and felt my head. Did I fall and hit my head? she asked. Did it hurt in one place more than in another? "We'll see how today goes," she said and then disappeared. Days passed. I do not recall how many. But every day Mama came to my bed and felt my head and said, "We'll see how today goes."

Then one day the pounding stopped. It just stopped. I did not take any medicine. Mama did not take me to the doctor. She just soothed my head each morning and said, "We'll see how today goes."

I do not remember going back to Aunt Lynn's that summer.

Don't You Know Birds Can't Talk?

In her later years, Mama had a mynah bird which she taught to smoke cigars, drink whiskey (so she could laugh when the bird slurred his speech), and say "Don't you know birds can't talk?" When someone came to visit, she would ask, "Did you see my mynah bird? They can talk, you know. He will repeat anything you say."

The unsuspecting guest would usually ask, "What should I say?"

Mama would answer, "Oh, you can say anything, and he will imitate you. Try, 'Pretty bird! Pretty bird!' He'll talk back to you."

Stepping close to the cage Mama's victim would say stupidly, "Pretty bird! Pretty bird!" To which the bird would respond, in what I was always sure was a "voice" dripping with sarcasm, "Don't you know birds can't talk?"

Mama also taught the bird to call my daddy. She and Daddy never slept together. When they moved to the house on the four-lane, after all but three of the children were gone, Mama slept downstairs with the bird and PomPom, her Pomeranian, and Daddy slept upstairs. Late one night when my husband and I were visiting, we heard a voice calling, "Roger! Roger!" Shortly, we heard Daddy coming downstairs, putting on his clothes en route, answering to the call of what turned out to be the bird.

Later, I asked Daddy why he came when he knew the odds were that it would be the bird. "Why do you demean yourself that way?"

Quietly and not exactly embarrassed, Daddy said, "I never

know if it is her calling me or the bird, so I go check just in case. Sometimes she wants me to make her some pudding during the night."

Mama was an adult-onset diabetic. She did not need to take insulin so long as she watched her diet closely. But watching her diet was not easy for a person with neglible self-discipline and an almost complete lack of interest in cooking (except on rare occasions when she could still cook a mean gumbo). Her idea of watching her diet was eating nothing but D'Zerta Chocolate Pudding with crunchy peanut butter mixed in (to give her something to bite into, she said) for months on end. (During another period she ate nothing but broccoli and cheese. That had nothing to do with being a diabetic, of course; it had to do with being obsessive/compulsive.) Mama said that her concoction tasted like Reece's Peanut Butter Cup, except that she always ate it hot, because she did not have enough self-control to wait until the pudding cooled and thickened. To keep the pantry well stocked, she bought D'Zerta Chocolate Pudding by the case and crunchy peanut butter in the largest size A and P carried—a sand pail designed for children to keep when they had eaten all the peanut butter.

Mama ate her homemade peanut butter cup three times a day and had more for snacks. Sometimes she craved it in the middle of the night. That is when she would call for Roger. He was loyal and devoted to her, in spite of all that had gone on through the years. That is why he always came when he heard his name called, no matter what the hour, even though he knew that it was probably the bird calling.

Mama managed some properties and houses belonging to the family with energy she had left over from teaching home ec in St. Martinsville. She used her house as her office. More accurately, she used her bedroom for an office. When tenants came to pay their rent, the mynah bird would welcome them and announce their presence: "Come on in. Miss Bernard! Miss

Bernard! Come on in. She's in her room." The tenants got so used to being greeted by the bird that they found themselves quite naturally talking back to it, sometimes leaving the rent on a table when Mama was not home.

One day the bird got out and flew a couple of miles to a sand pit. The talking bird was quite a novelty among the workers until they realized that he was saying, "Miss Bernard! Miss Bernard!" over and over. One of the workers went to the closest telephone, looked in the local directory for the Bernard who lived nearest the sand pit, called, and sure enough, it was Mama's mynah bird. Kevin, one of my brothers who was still home at the time, likes to say that the bird talked himself home.

Kevin also says that Mama taught the bird to wake him up in the morning for school by saying, "Kevin, seven o'clock. Time to get up. Go to School." Kevin swears that the bird did not wake him up on Saturday and Sunday mornings, but I don't believe that.

Mama's Gift

Mama's. Short for Mama's house. Like, "Sunday after mass we're going to Mama's house." Only we just said that we were going to Mama's.

Funny, now that I think about it, six years after her death, how everything seemed to belong to her. It was Mama's house and Mama's new Oldsmobile and Mama's trailer park and Mama's rent houses. PomPom was Mama's dog and Mama had a mynah bird and the baby grand piano in the living room was Mama's even though she had not played it in anyone's memory.

Daddy was there, too, of course. In his stock room doing something, counting things, reading his Bible. Staying out of her way mainly. His family, the Bernards, had land, cane fields, farms. They were proud people who traced their lineage from Nova Scotia and then back to sixteenth-century roots in Normandy. They had a live-in maid. As a child they seemed to me to be about as close to aristocracy as anything I could imagine. Whatever advantage this unlikely couple had in their early years of marriage, it was because of what Roger brought with him.

Mama's people, the Couvillions, were from Cottonport, Avoyelles Parish. They had nothing, and she brought nothing to the marriage, no property, no money, just her drive and her will and whatever needs and experiences made her the way she was. Still, nothing was ever Daddy's. Everything was Mama's.

Mama's was on the New Iberia highway, which most people called the "four-lane" because at that time the interstate had not been completed north of town and there was only one four-lane highway into and out of Lafayette. South of Mama's the four-lane by-passed Broussard, the quiet village which had been my haven in the stormy fourteenth year of life when I could no longer resist the bitter truth that Jeannine and Pookie forced on me, and I ran away to Aunt Lynn's for shelter and the warmth of someone who would be a mother to me. From Broussard, between thickly clustered sugar cane, the four-lane wound its way to New Iberia, Jeanerette, Morgan City, and other towns and communities which, even today, thirty years after I left the church and home, speak to me of my rich Acadian heritage.

It was Christmas, and like young families across the country, we were going home for the holidays. This biennial yuletide trek from WASP central Texas where my husband was in school—"*still* in school," Mama would say—was never easy for me. I would start getting nervous when we crossed the state line near Lake Charles, and I saw Spanish moss draped like shrouds over ancient limbs of mammoth live oaks and palmettos jutting out of the ground like nightmare spear-plants, forbidding entrance into the otherwise soft and tantalizing forest. We had been coming to Mama's every other Christmas for ten years—after Mama gave us permission to come home again—but it never got easier.

En route I critiqued everything I would say to her, imagining how she might reply and how I would respond to what she said. And what she would say then and how I would answer her. It was a game I played, thinking that I could somehow protect myself. It had never worked before but I played the game anyway.

This year I was more nervous than usual. It was because of the silver. Two Christmases earlier Mama had shocked me by giving me one of her most prized possessions, her sterling silver. At first I had resisted. But Mama would not be denied.

"Come on, now," Mama had said. "You take it. I gave Mike and Kevin money for down payments on their houses and I didn't give you anything. Come see. Look at that," she had said, opening the buffet drawer. "I chose demitasse spoons instead of salad forks. That's Cajun, huh?" Cajuns' love for strong coffee is notorious. Mello Joy dark roast, with or without chicory, must be sipped in small demitasse cups rather than swigged from clumsy mugs to be appreciated. In our home undersized spoons were more functional than decorative. Besides, we never ate salad.

The gift of the silver was only the most recent in a succession of gifts Mama and I had exchanged over the preceding decade. This peculiar mercenary way of relating to one another had begun in one of those awkward moments when neither of us knew what to say. I was wearing a thin, white "shawl" blouse at the time. It had pearlized buttons and an eight inch collar which gently caressed the neckline and was joined at the first button in front. Mama loved that blouse. That had been obvious since the first time she laid eyes on it. In the silence which suddenly descended on our conversation she blurted out, "I sure would like to have that blouse."

For a moment I was stunned. "What?" I asked.

"I sure would like to have that blouse," she repeated. "Can I have it?"

I did not know what to say. Her request, so blunt and so brazen, had taken me completely off guard. On our graduate-student income we could not afford many nice things, and my "shawl" was the only really nice blouse I had. I needed it. I loved it. She had no right to it. And she had no right making me feel that I ought to give it to her. Yet that is how I felt—that I ought to give it to her. Suddenly I was a child again, quivering inside, afraid Mama's wrath would come down on me. My degree meant nothing, the responsibilities I had shouldered meant nothing, the esteem in which I was held by my colleagues meant nothing. The only thing that mattered was that Mama wanted my blouse and that I ought to give it to her. So I did.

Quickly Mama went to her closet, flung open the door and, removing a full-length pale blue Christian Dior nightgown, said, "Do you want this?" "Sure," I replied. That is how it all began.

Over the years this strange ritual was repeated numerous

times. As often as not, the gifts we exchanged were items we had around the house. We did not shop for one another. We simply picked out from among the things we had something we thought the other would like.

It was not warm and endearing, this giving and receiving of gifts. It did not bring us together. It kept us apart. That is what it was designed to do. "Here. You want this?" was our substitute for genuine mother-daughter conversation, our way of not getting close, not showing our vulnerability. A pitcher and bowl made in ceramics class or a peignoir set guaranteed that neither of us would have to say, "I'm sorry. I love you. I hate you. I need you." We kept our emotions stilled, never revealing or exploring what or if we felt anything for each other.

I do not remember all the gifts I gave Mama or the gifts she gave me. But there was never a gift like the silver. It was extravagant, worth far more than any of the other presents we had exchanged. She must have known that I had nothing of equal value to give to her in return. Surely she knew that. More than anything in all of life I wanted to believe that she was offering me her silver as an act of love, an act of reconciliation. For the first time, the very first time, Mama was reaching out to me, trying in her typically crass way to bridge the gap that had separated us for so long. That is what I wanted to believe. But it was not that simple.

Mama had bought the silver with money given to her by one of her numerous lovers, a Mr. Begnaud who ran a grocery store in New Iberia. She had paid for it with twenty-dollar bills. There were place settings for seven rather than eight because their affair had broken up before she could buy the complete set. Nothing symbolized the shame I had felt all of my life more than that silver. How could I accept it as a gift? How could I display it in my home for my friends to see? If they said, "My, what beautiful silver. Has it been in your family long?" could I answer, "It was my mother's," and let it go at that? Or would I feel compelled to explain, so they would understand that I was not like her? Would not Mama's silver be a continual reminder of what I wanted so badly to forget?

But...why did Mama want me to have her silver? Was giving it to me her wordless confession of sin, her way of asking my forgiveness? Her penance? Was she trying to rid herself of the last tangible painful reminder of the life she had lived, a life that had made us the pariahs of the neighborhood—"les Bernard"—the brood of ten whom "decent" parents did not want their children playing with? Maybe it was understanding—rather than the cold condemnation she had felt from me for so long—that she wanted. Maybe it was approval. "It's OK, Mama. What you did was not wrong." Maybe that is what she imagined my acceptance of her gift would mean. But how could I know if she would not or could not say? And she would not or could not.

My mind was racing; my heart was confused. I could not know her motives. I scarcely knew my own. The only thing I was sure of was that giving her silver to me was very important to Mama and that somehow it revealed a deep, though terribly complicated love for me.

So I accepted from Mama the gift of her silver and allowed myself to feel something for her, something I had not done since I was a child. Not pity but an ever-so-cautious love. I was soon to be reminded how dangerous it could be to love Mama.

When my husband and I returned home after the holidays that year, I lined the middle drawer of the buffet with green velvet and lovingly placed my silver there. Every once in a while, when putting away dishes or polishing candlesticks or just walking through the dining room, I would open the drawer and gaze, sometimes through smiling tears, at what I had convinced myself was a sign of my mother's love for me.

The following spring Mama and Daddy came to Texas to visit us. They had not stayed with us before, and I was anxious for them to be comfortable. More importantly, I was anxious to build on the foundation that I felt had been laid the previous Christmas. My husband and I had closed in the garage, converting it into a den/playroom. I planned for Mama and Daddy to sleep on the hide-a-bed, though I knew that they had not slept together for years. The meals were planned, the groceries bought, and the house cleaned. There was nothing left to do but await their arrival, which I did with great anticipation.

Mama and Daddy had been in our home less than two hours when she announced, "I came to get my silver. I want to take it back with me."

I thought I was hearing things. "What? You gave me that silver."

"Oh no," she said, "I didn't give it to you. I said you could keep it for a long, long time. I didn't give it to you." There was determination in her voice and a hint of nervousness, as though she had anticipated this confrontation, but there was no anger.

I felt my face suddenly pale. An old familiar fear returned to my stomach. Inside my head, I began rehearsing lines I had no intention of saying aloud. "You can't do this to me. You can't take it back. I need it." Suddenly, to my dismay, the inner words were given voice, and I said more forcefully than I had ever spoken to her, "You *gave* me that silver."

"No," she countered with greater force. "I did not give it to you. I said you could keep it for a long time, and now I want it back." By now she was standing. Her graying red hair seemed to be on fire. She had a way of standing when she wanted to intimidate her opponent. She would pull in her chin and thrust her chest upward, cocking her head slightly to one side, making her seem a foot taller than the five foot two she actually was. Her eyebrows would tighten over her eyes, and her voice, always harsh and flat, would become shrill and loud. And I would quiver inside.

Frantic, I turned to Daddy and pleaded, "Daddy, you

remember. She gave it to me." He simply sat there with that sheepish expression I had seen so many times. I should have known he would not take my side if it meant taking her on. He said limply, "Oh, chere, I don't know anything about that."

I turned again to Mama and said in desperation, "You know you gave it to me. You know you did."

This time she made no response. She just looked at me sternly as though the issue were settled. Angry and crushed, I went to the dining room, opened the middle drawer of the buffet, gathered the silver in my arms, returned to the den, and threw it on the sofa beside her. Within fifteen minutes she and Daddy were on their way back to Lafayette. As they drove away, I watched and cried tears drawn from a well so deep it would be years before I would begin to fathom its darkened depths.

The next day the phone rang, and my husband answered. "It's long distance," he said. "It's Ethel." What could she want? How could she call me after what she did to me? The pain was still fresh and sharp, but I allowed myself to wonder whether she was calling to apologize for her selfishness and thoughtlessness. On the way to the telephone my mind delighted in contemplating alternately the return of the silver and the renewal of a relationship with Mama which had ended so cruelly.

"I wonder if you would give me the mate to the gold bowl-bottom lamp that you gave me a couple of years ago," Mama said. "I have rearranged the living room and bought a new sofa and, if I had both lamps, the room would really pull together."

The audacity. The shamelessness. "No, I don't want to give it to you."

"I really would like to have the set," she said. "It doesn't do either of us any good to have just one."

"No," I said firmly, trembling with anger. "I like my lamp."

"I will pay you for it," she said. "Buy yourself a new lamp and send me the mate to the one I have."

"You don't know how much lamps cost," I said. "It has been

a long time since you have bought a lamp. It could cost a hundred dollars."

"It doesn't matter what it costs," she replied. "I want the mate."

By now the stress was incredibly high. "No," I said, fairly shouting into the phone.

"It's the silver, isn't it?" she said.

Of course, it was the silver. But I did not dare let her know how much it had meant to me. I could not allow her to sense my vulnerability. I was weak from the tension of the conversation, worn down by the challenge of someone who had always been larger than life to me. But I managed to lie once more convincingly and with feeling. "No, Mama. I really like my lamp." Maybe it was my strength. Maybe it was my weakness. Maybe she sensed my pain and did not want to hurt me any more. Whatever the reason, Mama backed off. I could hear it in her silence.

Then Mama asked me for the black half-slip she had given me a year earlier, and I said I would send it to her.

As we passed the airport, Mama's came into view. It was not the house I grew up in, the house of painful memories on General Mouton Street. It was the house Mama and Daddy built after all but three of the children were gone. The two-story, slope-roofed brick house stood between massive oaks which dripped with moss, their thick, strong arms offering shade to the entire yard. The grass was deep green and lush. A feather-leafed, pink-blossomed mimosa stood just outside the door. The scene which lay before us as we pulled into the driveway would have suggested peacefulness and gentility if it were not for the embarrassing eyesore Mama had made of her property. On the back side of the lot, arranged in a row along a dirt road which was packed with tiny white shells, were several small, ramshackle rent houses which Mama had bought and moved from town in her never-ending effort to make money. Across the road from the rent houses, virtually in Mama's yard, were fourteen dented, rusting manufactured homes, which is what they were called after they were called mobile homes, which is what they were called after they were called trailer houses, which is what Mama called them because, she insisted, that is what they were.

The most prominent feature of Mama's living room was a tall cedar Christmas tree, wonderfully decorated, its top crowned with an angel. It was beautiful. So beautiful that it seemed it should be in someone else's house. For in the later years of my childhood and youth we had only a small aluminum tree, three-and-a-half feet tall and painted gold. The marvelous tree which now stood beneath the overhanging balcony took me back before those bad days to a time of dreaming innocence, long before I heard the whispers of neighbors and felt the red blush of shame on my cheeks. In that beatific day we had a "real" Christmas tree.

When I knelt to place my armload of presents under the tree, I noticed a neatly wrapped rectangular box on which there was an envelope labeled, "For Rosie." My interest was piqued, but I placed my gifts under the tree and stood, for it was not time to exchange presents. Mama, who had welcomed us in her predictably stiff way and was still lagging behind near the door, walked quickly to the tree, picked up the box and gave it to me, all without saying a word.

The box was heavy, the weight evenly distributed. I did not have to open it to know that Mama's silver was inside. My heart beat fast and my eyes filled with tears as I removed the card from the envelope which bore my name. On the card was a handwritten note: "This time it is for keeps. Love, Mama."

For a moment we did not speak. But the silence was not empty; it was full—full of feelings too deep for words, "sounds which cannot be uttered." Suddenly, I no longer wanted the silver. I was sorry that I had caused such trouble for her. Clearly, the silver still had deep meaning for her, though I could only guess what that meaning might be. I made a move to give the box back to her, but Mama said quietly, "No, this time it really is for keeps." I reached out and hugged Mama. Her back was rigid, the muscles in her shoulders were taut, and her smile was strained, but it did not matter. I understood for the first time that Mama loved as much as she could—it was not enough, I have wished for more, longed for more, but it was all she could do—and she expressed her love the only way she knew how.

Mama's silver is in the buffet in my dining room now, nestled in the green velvet which I had never removed. To my dinner guests I say simply, "This was my mother's silver. See the small spoons? Cajuns love strong coffee, you know. So, she chose demitasse spoons instead of salad forks. Mama gave it to me before she died." I let it go at that.

God's Gracious Clover

Aunt Lynn died in the winter of 1990, after a slow decline which left her slight and stooped, with frightened eyes peering out of a pale, sunken face. Eunice—Nanaine Eune, scurrying, chattering, funny, humpback Eune—followed in March. Ma'Lou had died a year before. Daddy was in a nursing home. Mama had been dead for four years. The older generation was passing away, taking with them all the fleshly reminders of my past.

I had been in treatment for severe clinical depression in North Carolina for a month when Aunt Lynn died and was unable to make the thousand-mile trip to Lafayette and deal with whatever demons might be loosed by her funeral. It was a wise decision not to attend, though in reality it was no decision at all. By the time Eune died, I had reached a plateau—except that I did not know it was a plateau at the time, preferring to think that my plunge into darkness had been more short-lived than the psychiatrists had predicted—and felt that I was up to whatever such a trip might bring.

I had visited Lafayette many times over the thirty years that had passed since I left home. But only once in all those years, only once, had I returned to 326 General Mouton, the site of the bitter memories of my childhood. It was not as though I considered the possibility and ruled it out because it was inconvenient or because there was not time. The possibility just never came up. I never thought of it. It isn't hard to imagine why.

My single visit to the house of my growing-up years had been a mixture of pleasure and pain. Several years earlier Mama and Daddy had moved to the trailer park on the four-lane and had sold the house on General Mouton to a fraternity of the University of Southwestern Louisiana. Greek letters were painted over the front door. The very thought that the house in which I spent the entirety of my childhood and a significant portion of my youth, the house in which my brothers and sisters and I played and imagined and worked and survived, the house which, in spite of all else it stood for, represented the single visible, architectural anchor in my life, had been turned over to a fraternity was almost more than I could bear. I had visions of holes in the walls and knee-deep debris. But, then, why did I expect other people— especially college students—to take better care of the house than we had? The students lived down to my expectations. For the most part, the interior of the house was barely recognizable; the fraternity boys had trashed the house almost beyond recognition. Nothing was the same, the furniture, the color of the paint, nothing. The rooms were where they were supposed to be, but everything else was different. The greatest shock was that the house was so small. The bedrooms, the bathroom, the living room—could ten people really have lived there?

My greatest surprise, and my greatest joy, was the discovery that the red and white checkered tile floor Mama had laid in the kitchen—with my "help"—was still there. I felt a strange sense of pride that something she and I had done together, as partners, had survived the generation of my brothers and sisters and several generations of college students. I could see Mama on her knees spreading the black tar paper and then setting each square of tile in place—symetrically so that the red tiles and white tiles touched only at the corners like a checkerboard—with a glue I can smell to this day. I remembered how beautiful that floor was and how, when the project was finished, we stood and looked at it and felt proud.

This bittersweet experience had been my only acquaintance with my childhood home for thirty years, until the first spring of my darkness when I knew that I had to return yet again.

My husband wanted to know why. Why did I have to go

back? "What do you expect to find?" he asked. I was not sure. I only knew that I had to go. Maybe I had missed something when I was there before, some memory that would make everything make sense, like a missing piece of a puzzle left on a table to be worked on when there is more time. But there was no more time. I hurt now, and I needed to know now. I could not rid myself of the feeling that there was something in that house, in its walls or in its foundations, something that I had to confront and conquer. That is what I would do. I would attack that little house, smash it, make sure that there was nothing left in the ceilings or floors to infiltrate my mind in some deep sleep of night from which I would awaken with screams and tears. The sheer physicalness of the house was my focus. I would look in every room, open every closet door. If there was a demon there, I would find it. And I would deal with it. I was as angry and as determined as Mama ever was, angrier and more determined than I had ever been.

So, after Eune's funeral, I asked Kevin, my brother, to drive me to General Mouton Street, taking the route I took each day when I walked home from Mt. Carmel High School in the ninth and tenth grades: through the intersection of Johnson and Oak, with Kellar's Bakery on one corner and Borden's Ice Cream on the other, right on General Gardner, past Grandma's house, and then left on General Mouton. I had it planned. I would ask the current occupants (the fraternity had moved out several years before) if I could look around. I would explain that this had been my house. That it still was my house, in a way. They were just living there, these people. Would you please let me see my house?

Surprisingly very little in the neighborhood had changed. The houses, the sidewalks, the landmarks seen only by walking children, were still there. It felt very familiar and deceptively comfortable, just as it had in my childhood. I could easily imagine myself as a brown-skirted freshman once again, walking home after school, an impressive stack of books and papers under my left arm, my upper body leaning to the right as a counterweight. The warmth of the relived moment was qualified only by the tension which I could feel rising in anticipation of I knew not what.

Our house would be on the right. First, the house where the Kennedys used to live, then the Leblancs, the Toneys, and the two-story rent house that belonged to the Toneys. Then our house. It would be white with a dark roof. It would have a screened-in front porch, but the vine which grew and covered the porch in the summer, shading it, providing a natural privacy barrier for me, Jeannine, Pookie, and our dates, would be no more than a sprout now. The zinnias Pookie and I planted by the front steps would be there. There would be a pear tree in the back yard and a sagging clothesline with more clothes than pins. The garage door would be open, and I would be able to see Daddy's Standard Coffee panel truck and hear Mama telling us to get out there and help Daddy load up for his route. There would be soft green fern under the house—forboding yet inviting, a safe hiding place for a ten-year-old who saw more than she understood.

The car slowed to a stop, and I looked, confused, to my right out the window. For a moment the scene did not register in my mind. It was as though we had skipped suddenly into a strange, unknown neighborhood. Kevin knew, but he didn't tell me. The house was gone. Physically, literally gone. The sidewalk was there but the steps and the porch were gone. The twin-rutted driveway, paved with tiny white shells, omnipresent in the driveways of south Louisiana, was there, but the garage was gone. The brick pillars on which the house rested were there, but the house—the house with which I desperately needed to make peace—was gone. Charlie Magnon, who lived across the street when I was a girl, had grown up and bought it and moved it somewhere. Kevin didn't know where.

"Go on," I told Kevin shakily as I got out of the car. "I'll walk to Michael's house when I'm through."

Kevin drove away and left me looking into an unexpected emptiness. The sight of the houseless lot, seeming so much smaller now that the house was gone, had a stunning physical effect on me. It was as though someone had hit me in the stomach. I clasped my arms across my abdomen and fell to my knees on the sidewalk. I felt weak and unsteady and remained in a hunched position for several minutes. When my head cleared, I looked up and let the sight sink in: over the entire lot, between the ruts of the driveway, lapping at the base of the brick pillars, was grass. Thick green grass.

Ours had been the only house in the neighborhood which had no grass. We had played in a desert of black dirt which extended from the sidewalk to the fern under the house. Now, where once there had been a house with no grass, there was grass with no house. Where once there was only dirt, now there was a carpet of rich, deep St. Augustine grass.

Bamboo was thick on the right side of the lot as it had been in my youth, but now it grew across the back of the property as well. When I was a child, there was no barrier between our yard and the yard of Mr. Chaplin who lived behind us. Now the bamboo formed an impenetrable reedy fence, and the property on Mr. Chaplin's side was thick with undergrowth. No matter. The yard—*my* yard—was blanketed with wonderful grass and protected by a wall of bamboo.

Then, from my kneeling position on the sidewalk, I saw... I saw a priest, wearing a cream-colored robe and a red stole, holding a gold holy water sprinkler in his hand. The container was filled to overflowing; beads formed, rolled down its rounded surface, and dropped to the sidewalk. Without looking my way, the priest lifted his right hand and with the flick of his wrist splashed water as far into the yard as he could, and as he did, he said, "I forgive you. I forgive you. God bless you. I forgive you." He stepped on to the carpet and walked single-mindedly around the yard, bathing it in holy water and pronouncing everywhere he stepped, "I forgive you. I forgive you. God bless you. I forgive you."

When the entire lawn was soaked and I along with it, the priest walked past me and disappeared, and I was left staring at a miracle: everywhere the drops of holy water had fallen, beautiful, round, white clover had sprung up, a testimony to God's healing spirit and a loving gift of God's grace.

I brushed the mercy drops from my cheeks and, leaning forward, grasped a handful of soft, cool clover and put it in my purse. Then I got up and walked away.

I don't need to go home again.